Investigate Science

Use Your Senses

by Melissa Stewart

Content Adviser: Jan Jenner, Ph.D.

Science Adviser: Terrence E. Young Jr., M.Ed.,
M.L.S., Jefferson Parish (La.) Public Schools

Reading Adviser: Rosemary G. Palmer, Ph.D.,
Department of Literacy, College of Education,
Boise State University

COMPASS POINT BOOKS MINNEAPOLIS, MINNESOTA

Compass Point Books
3109 West 50th St., #115
Minneapolis, MN 55410

Visit Compass Point Books on the Internet at *www.compasspointbooks.com* or e-mail your request to *custserv@compasspointbooks.com*

Photographs ©: Gary Sundermeyer, cover (middle & bottom left), 1 (bottom left); PhotoDisc, cover background, 1, 7 (right), 12, 24; Brand X Pictures, 4, 7 (left), 15, 21, 22; Stockbyte, 5 (top), 17 (bottom); Creatas, 5 (bottom); Gary Milburn/Tom Stack & Associates, 6; Tom & Dee Ann McCarthy/Corbis, 8; Fotopic/Index Stock Imagery, 9; Corbis, 10; Tony Rinaldo/Index Stock Imagery, 11; Gregg Andersen, 13 (all), 17 (top), 18 (all), 20, 25 (all); Laura Doss/Corbis, 14; Image Source, 16; EyeWire, 23.

Creative Director: Terri Foley
Managing Editor: Catherine Neitge
Editors: Nadia Higgins, Christianne C. Jones
Photo Researcher: Svetlana Zhurkina
Designer: The Design Lab
Illustrator: Jeffrey Scherer
Educational Consultant: Diane Smolinski

Library of Congress Cataloging-in-Publication Data
Stewart, Melissa.
Use your senses / by Melissa Stewart.
  p. cm. — (Investigate science)
Summary: Introduces the characteristics and importance of the five senses through text, illustrations, and activities.
Includes bibliographical references and index.
  ISBN 0-7565-0636-0 (hardcover)
1. Senses and sensation—Juvenile literature. [1. Senses and sensation.] I. Title. II. Series.
QP434.S747 2004
612.8—dc22   2003022718

Note to Readers: To learn about our five senses, scientists do experiments. They write about everything they observe. They make charts and drawings.

This book will help you study the five senses the way a scientist does. To get started, you will need to get a notebook and a pencil.

In the Doing More section in the back of the book, you will find step-by-step instructions for some more fun science experiments and activities.

In this book, words that are defined in the glossary are in **bold** the first time they appear in the text.

Table of Contents

As you read this book, be on the lookout for these special symbols:

Ask an Adult — Ask an adult for help.

Doing More — Turn to the back of the book for another activity.

See Explanation — Go to page 30 for an explanation to a question.

Making Sense of Senses

Find a mirror and look closely at your face. Draw a picture of everything you see.

Think about your eyes, ears, skin, nose, and tongue. Each of these five parts is related to one of your five **senses.** Your eyes see. Your ears hear. Your skin senses touch. What does your nose do? What about your tongue?

Your amazing senses help you understand what's going on around you. Let's test your senses with some experiments. You might be surprised by what your senses can do!

You use your five senses to gather information about the world around you.

Your senses alert you to dangers such as fires.

Think About How Your Senses Help You

Why are your five senses so important? They help you stay safe. If a building is on fire, your eyes see flames, your nose smells smoke, and your skin feels heat. You run away!

Your senses also let you enjoy the world around you. Your tongue tastes a tart apple. Your ears hear your favorite song. Your nose smells a fragrant flower.

Make a chart like the one shown below. Think about all the ways your senses help you stay safe and enjoy the world. Fill in the chart with your own examples.

	Eyes	Nose	Tongue	Skin	Ears
Staying Safe	see fire	smells smoke			
Enjoying the World			tastes an apple		hear music

Your senses
let you enjoy
the things in
your world.

Your brain decides how to react to the information your senses collect.

How Do You Respond to Your Sensors?

Your ears, eyes, nose, tongue, and skin are always working. They have **sensors** that collect information about everything around you. The sensors send messages to your brain. Then your brain tells your body how to act. When your brain gets a message that your skin feels something hot, it tells your arms and legs to move away.

Draw pictures showing what your brain tells your body to do when:

- your ear sensors hear a car horn blasting right behind you.

- your nose sensors smell a cookie.

- your eye sensors see a ball coming at you.

Sometimes, when they become tired or blocked, your sensors can become unreliable. Turn to page 26 for an activity that shows how your sensors can trick you.

Which sensors is this boy responding to?

Doing More

9

Your senses are always working together.

Focus Your Senses

You can use many senses at once. Which of your five senses do you use when you bounce a ball? How about when you play with a puppy?

Your senses send a lot of information to your brain. So your brain is always deciding what to focus on. Right now, you are focusing on this book. You are blocking out most of the sounds around you. If an alarm went off, though, you'd look up to see what was happening.

The next time you go for a walk outside, make a list of everything you see, hear, smell, and touch. Do not taste anything during your walk.

Put on a blindfold and ask a friend to help you take the same walk again. Do you sense anything new? Why? See page 30 for an explanation.

See Explanation

What you need:
• a blindfold

How many different things can you sense on a walk outside?

Seeing and Hearing

How Does Darkness Affect Your Sight?

What you need:
• 3–4 sheets of construction paper, each one a different color

Tonight, spread out some sheets of colored construction paper on a table or the floor in your room. Then turn off all the lights, and look at the sheets of construction paper. Can you tell which pieces are red, blue, or green? Now look around your room. Can you see the colors in your bedspread, rug, and curtains?

When it's dark, you see things in shades of gray, not in full color. That's because your eyes have two kinds of sensors—**cones** and **rods.** Cones can sense colors, but they only work when there's enough light. Rods don't need a lot of light to work, but rods can only see shades of gray. Rods are important for sensing shapes and movements, not colors.

Think About It!

The black circle in the center of your eye is called a **pupil.** The pupil is where light enters the eye. When it gets dark, your pupil gets bigger. Can you guess why? See page 30 for an answer.

? See Explanation

12

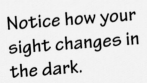

Notice how your sight changes in the dark.

Why Do You Need Two Eyes?

Your eyes both see the same things, and yet you have two of them. Why? To find out, shut one eye and try to play catch. Is it easy or hard?

When you look at a ball with just one eye, it's hard to tell how far away it is. That's because each eye sees the ball from a slightly different angle. When your brain combines the images from each eye, you can tell exactly where the ball is.

What you need:
• a ball

Did You Know?

Sometimes you want to use just one eye. Think about what eye you'd use to take a picture or to look through a telescope. You always choose one eye over the other. Just as people are right-handed or left-handed, people are "right-eyed" or "left-eyed."

You need both eyes to judge the distance of a ball.

15

Did You Know?

If you were a rabbit or a cat, you could turn your ears in the direction of a sound to hear it better. Most people can't move their ears at all, but some can wiggle their ears a little. What about you?

Why Do You Need Two Ears?

Having two ears is important, too. Cover one ear with your hand, shut your eyes, and listen. Try to guess where sounds are coming from. Is it easy or hard?

Having two ears helps your brain figure out where sounds are coming from. If a fire engine's siren sounds louder in your left ear, your brain knows the sound is coming from the left.

Having two ears lets you know which way to turn your head when somebody calls your name. It helps you find a ringing phone. How else does having two ears help you?

For another activity about sound, see page 27.

Doing More

How does your hearing change when you cover one ear?

You know which way to look when someone calls you because you have two ears.

17

Test your sense of smell. Then compare your results with a friend.

Smell, Taste, and Touch

Test Your Sense of Smell

Ask an Adult

Ask an adult to cut up some fruits and vegetables in another room. Now mark a spot with masking tape. Put on a blindfold or shut your eyes, and stand there. Have a friend choose a food and slowly walk toward you until you can name it. Use more tape to mark the spot where your friend stopped. This tape shows where you began to smell the food. Write down the name of the food on the tape.

Do this again with all the pieces of food in the other room. When you're done, measure the distances between where you stood and each of the other markers. Write down your results in a chart like the one pictured here. Which food was hardest to smell? Which was easiest?

Now have your friend try the experiment. Complete the chart. Which of you has a better sense of smell? How can you tell? See page 30 for an answer.

See Explanation

What you need:
- 4–6 different kinds of fruits and vegetables, cut up
- masking tape
- blindfold (optional)
- measuring tape

	Tony	Omar
Lemon	5 inches (12 ½ cm)	
Tomato	6 inches (15 cm)	
Cucumber	1 foot (30 cm)	
Pepper	4 feet (1.2 meters)	
Orange	10 feet (3 meters)	

See How Smell Affects Taste

Now have your friend shut his or her eyes, or use a blindfold. Hold a piece of onion near your friend's nose with one hand. With the other hand, feed him or her a piece of apple. Then ask your friend what he or she just ate. Are you surprised by the answer? The way a food smells has a lot to do with how it tastes. The strong onion smell may have overpowered the apple's taste.

Taste and smell are so closely related, the two can get mixed up.

Think About It!

Why can't you taste food very well when you have a stuffy nose? See page 30 for an answer. **See Explanation**

21

Did You Know?

Your tongue senses more than just taste. It also feels food. It tells your brain potato chips are crispy, while ice cream is cool and creamy.

22

How Does Saliva Affect Your Sense of Taste?

Look in a mirror and stick out your tongue. Do you see lots of little white bumps on it? Those bumps have sensors inside them. These sensors send taste messages to your brain.

Dry off the tip of your tongue with a napkin. Then sprinkle a little sugar on it. What do you taste? Now pull your tongue back in your mouth and wet it with **saliva.** Put more sugar on the tip of your tongue. Do you taste a difference?

Saliva helps break down food so your taste sensors can work. When your tongue is covered with more saliva, sugar tastes sweeter.

See page 28 for another activity about your taste sensors.

What you need:
- *a napkin*
- *sugar*

Bumps on your tongue are full of taste sensors.

23

Blind people use their sensitive fingertips to read braille.

Which Areas of Your Body Are Most Sensitive to Touch?

What you need:
• tweezers

Rub the tips of your fingers on a sheet of paper. Now rub your elbow on the paper. You can feel the paper better with your fingers. Touch sensors are all over your skin, but some body parts, such as fingers, have more sensors than others.

To find out what areas have the most sensors, gently press the tips of tweezers on different parts of your body. Try your hands, face, arms, fingers, legs, feet, and toes. Have a friend test your back.

Draw a picture of your body showing where you could feel both tips and where you could feel just one tip. Go to page 30, and read the list of the body's most sensitive parts. Does your picture match this list? On page 29, you'll find another activity about touch sensors.

Doing More

Now that you've tested your senses, you know how well they work. Pay attention to all the ways you can see, hear, smell, taste, and touch. Your five senses let you explore your world.

Use tweezers to test your sense of touch. Then record your results.

25

Trick Your Sensors

What you need:
- a green apple
- a sheet of white paper
- orange juice
- toothpaste and a toothbrush

On page 9, you learned that the sensors in your ears, eyes, nose, tongue, and skin are hard at work. Sometimes they have trouble doing their job, though. The following experiments will show you what happens when sensors get tired or are blocked.

1. Stare at a green apple for about a minute. Now look at a white piece of paper. Are you surprised by what you see? You see a red apple because the eye sensors that see green are very tired. The eyes sensors that see red take over for a second or two.

2. Walk into a room you haven't been in for a while, and take a deep breath. What do you smell? After you've been in the room for 10 minutes, take another breath. What do you smell now? After 10 minutes, your nose sensors got used to the smells in the room. The smells don't seem as strong as they did before.

3. Drink a glass of orange juice. Now go brush your teeth, and then drink a little more juice. Does the juice taste different? Toothpaste blocks the sweetness of juice for a while, so you only taste the sour and bitter flavors.

See Sound Waves at Work

On page 17, you learned that having two ears helps you pinpoint sounds. A sound is made when something vibrates, or moves back and forth very quickly. You hear buzzing when a bee beats its wings, and you hear music when someone plucks a guitar's strings. Sound travels in invisible waves, but you can see the power of those waves by doing this experiment.

Ask an Adult

1. Have an adult cut a small, square piece of plastic wrap, and place it over a large, plastic container.

2. Secure the plastic wrap around the container with a rubber band.

3. Sprinkle a few pieces of crispy rice cereal on top of the plastic wrap.

4. Hold the lid of a metal pot a few inches away from the plastic container. Now bang on the metal lid with a wooden spoon. What happens to the cereal?

Sound waves are traveling away from the metal lid. The waves travel through the air like ripples in a pond. When the waves reach your ears, you hear a noise. When the waves reach the cereal, the cereal moves.

What you need:
• plastic wrap
• plastic container
• rubber band
• crispy rice cereal
• metal lid
• wooden spoon

27

What you need:
- 4 bowls
- unsweetened grapefruit juice
- vinegar
- warm water
- salt
- sugar
- a spoon for stirring
- 4 Q-tips

Find the Four Taste Areas of Your Tongue

On page 23, you learned that you have taste sensors on the top of your tongue. Some of them sense sweet foods, while others sense sour, salty, or bitter flavors. Each kind of sensor is grouped together on an area of the tongue. To find where the four different kinds of taste sensors are, try this experiment.

1. Label four bowls 1, 2, 3, and 4. Add unsweetened grapefruit juice to Bowl 1, vinegar to Bowl 2, and warm water to Bowls 3 and 4.

2. Add a little salt to Bowl 3 and a little sugar to Bowl 4. Stir both mixtures until you can't see the sugar or salt in the water anymore.

3. Dip a Q-tip in Bowl 1, and dab it on different parts of your tongue. Only your bitter taste sensors will be able to taste the grapefruit juice. Can you tell where on your tongue your bitter taste sensors are?

4. Rinse out your mouth with plain water, and repeat Step 3 with the sour (vinegar) mixture. Then try the salty (salt water) and sweet (sugar water) mixtures, rinsing out your mouth between each one.

5. Draw a picture of your tongue, and label where each kind of taste sensor is located. (Hint: Most taste sensors are on the sides, back, and tip of your tongue.) Compare your picture to the one on page 30. Were you able to tell where your taste sensors are?

Identify Objects by Touch

Just as your tongue has four kinds of taste sensors, your skin has four kinds of touch sensors. Some sensors can detect heat, while others sense cold, pain, or pressure. However, while your taste sensors each have their own areas on your tongue, your touch sensors work together on all parts of your skin.

On page 25, you learned that fingers have more touch sensors than most other parts of the body. Let's see if all those sensors can help you identify an object without looking at it.

1. Place a variety of objects in a bag that you can't see through. Try to find a lot of different things, such as a sponge, an orange, raisins, a hairbrush, or a leaf.

2. Ask a friend to reach in the bag without looking inside it. Have your friend describe the objects. Are they hard or soft? Hot or cold? Light or heavy? Smooth or rough? Can your friend guess what he or she is touching? Ask your friend to fill another bag, and you try to guess what's inside it.

3. For an extra challenge, put on a pair of thin gloves, and try the activity again.

What you need:
- a bag that you can't see through
- 5–7 objects that feel different from each other
- thin gloves (optional)

Explanations to Questions

Outdoor Walk *(from page 11)*

By shutting your eyes, your brain didn't have to keep track of everything you saw. It could focus more on what you were hearing, smelling, and feeling.

Pupils *(from Think About It! page 12)*

The pupil gets bigger to let in more light so you can see better in the dark. When you enter bright light, the pupil gets smaller again.

Smelling Fruit *(from page 19)*

The one who can smell the most foods from farthest away has a better sense of smell—at least for today.

Stuffy Nose *(from Think About It! page 21)*

Your stuffy nose blocks your sense of smell. Your nose can't help your tongue bring out the full flavor of your food.

Body Parts Most Sensitive to Touch *(from page 25)*

Fingers

Lips

Neck

Feet

Tip of tongue

Tip of nose

The middle of your back is the area least sensitive to touch.

Taste Areas on the Tongue

(from page 28)
How well does this picture match the one you drew?

Glossary

cones—eye sensors that see colors in bright light

pupil—the black center of the eye; the pupil gets bigger and smaller to let in or keep out light

rods—eye sensors that see shapes and movements in dim light

saliva—another word for spit

senses—powers, such as seeing or hearing, that you use to collect information about the world

sensors—the parts of your eyes, ears, nose, tongue, and skin that send messages about your surroundings to your brain

To Find Out More

At the Library

Nettleton, Pamela Hill. *Look, Listen, Taste, Touch, and Smell*. Minneapolis: Picture Window Books, 2004.

Scott, Janine. *Our Senses*. Minneapolis: Compass Point Books, 2003.

Sweeney, Joan. *Me and My Senses*. New York: Crown Publishers, 2003.

Williamson, Sarah. *Fun with My 5 Senses: Activities to Build Learning Readiness*. Charlotte, Vt.: Williamson Publishing, 1998.

On the Web

For more information on the **senses**, use FactHound to track down Web sites related to this book.

1. Go to *www.facthound.com*
2. Type in a search word related to this book or this book ID: 0756506360.
3. Click on the *Fetch It* button.

Your trusty FactHound will fetch the best Web sites for you!

31

Index

About the Author

Melissa Stewart earned a bachelor's degree in biology from Union College and a master's degree in science and environmental journalism from New York University. After editing children's science books for nearly a decade, she decided to focus on writing. She has written more than 50 science books for children and contributed articles to *ChemMatters*, *Instructor*, *MATH*, *National Geographic World*, *Natural New England*, *Odyssey*, *Ranger Rick*, *Science World*, and *Wild Outdoor World*. She also teaches writing workshops and develops hands-on science programs for schools near her home in Northborough, Massachusetts.